Fre

C000004938

by Iain Gray

Lang**Syne**

PUBLISHING

WRITING *to* REMEMBER

LangSyne

PUBLISHING

WRITING *to* REMEMBER

79 Main Street, Newtongrange,
Midlothian EH22 4NA
Tel: 0131 344 0414   Fax: 0845 075 6085
E-mail: info@lang-syne.co.uk
www.langsyneshop.co.uk

Design by Dorothy Meikle
Printed by Ricoh Print Scotland
© Lang Syne Publishers Ltd 2013

ISBN 978-1-85217-510-8

Freeman

MOTTO:
Neither rashly nor timidly
(and)
Free and bold
(and)
Liberty and my native soil.

CREST:
A rearing demi-lion rampant
holding a golden diamond-shaped
lozenge in its paws.

NAME variations include:
Freman
Friman
Fryman

Chapter one:

The origins of popular surnames

by George Forbes and Iain Gray

If you don't know where you came from, you won't know where you're going is a frequently quoted observation and one that has a particular resonance today when there has been a marked upsurge in interest in genealogy, with increasing numbers of people curious to trace their family roots.

Main sources for genealogical research include census returns and official records of births, marriages and deaths – and the key to unlocking the detail they contain is obviously a family surname, one that has been 'inherited' and passed from generation to generation.

No matter our station in life, we all have a surname – but it was not until about the middle of the fourteenth century that the practice of being identified by a particular surname became commonly established throughout the British Isles.

Previous to this, it was normal for a person to be identified through the use of only a forename.

But as population gradually increased and there were many more people with the same forename, surnames were adopted to distinguish one person, or community, from another.

Many common English surnames are patronymic in origin, meaning they stem from the forename of one's father – with 'Johnson,' for example, indicating 'son of John.'

It was the Normans, in the wake of their eleventh century conquest of Anglo-Saxon England, a pivotal moment in the nation's history, who first brought surnames into usage – although it was a gradual process.

For the Normans, these were names initially based on the title of their estates, local villages and chateaux in France to distinguish and identify these landholdings.

Such grand descriptions also helped enhance the prestige of these warlords and generally glorify their lofty positions high above the humble serfs slaving away below in the pecking order who had only single names, often with Biblical connotations as in Pierre and Jacques.

The only descriptive distinctions among the peasantry concerned their occupations, like 'Pierre the swineherd' or 'Jacques the ferryman.'

Roots of surnames that came into usage in England not only included Norman-French, but also Old French, Old Norse, Old English, Middle English, German, Latin, Greek, Hebrew and the Gaelic languages of the Celts.

The Normans themselves were originally Vikings, or 'Northmen', who raided, colonised and eventually settled down around the French coastline.

The had sailed up the Seine in their longboats in 900AD under their ferocious leader Rollo and ruled the roost in north eastern France before sailing over to conquer England in 1066 under Duke William of Normandy – better known to posterity as William the Conqueror, or King William I of England.

Granted lands in the newly-conquered England, some of their descendants later acquired territories in Wales, Scotland and Ireland – taking not only their own surnames, but also the practice of adopting a surname, with them.

But it was in England where Norman rule and custom first impacted, particularly in relation to the adoption of surnames.

This is reflected in the famous *Domesday Book*, a massive survey of much of England and Wales, ordered by William I, to determine who owned what, what it was worth and therefore how much they were liable to pay in taxes to the voracious Royal Exchequer.

Completed in 1086 and now held in the National Archives in Kew, London, 'Domesday' was an Old English word meaning 'Day of Judgement.'

This was because, in the words of one contemporary chronicler, "its decisions, like those of the Last Judgement, are unalterable."

It had been a requirement of all those English landholders – from the richest to the poorest – that they identify themselves for the purposes of the survey and for future reference by means of a surname.

This is why the *Domesday Book*, although written in Latin as was the practice for several centuries with both civic and ecclesiastical records, is an invaluable source for the early appearance of a wide range of English surnames.

Several of these names were coined in connection with occupations.

These include Baker and Smith, while Cooks, Chamberlains, Constables and Porters were to be found carrying out duties in large medieval households.

The church's influence can be found in names such as Bishop, Friar and Monk while the popular name of Bennett derives from the late fifth to mid-sixth century Saint Benedict, founder of the Benedictine order of monks.

The early medical profession is represented by Barber, while businessmen produced names that include Merchant and Sellers.

Down at the village watermill, the names that cropped up included Millar/Miller, Walker and Fuller, while other self-explanatory trades included Cooper, Tailor, Mason and Wright.

Even the scenery was utilised as in Moor, Hill, Wood and Forrest – while the hunt and the chase supplied names that include Hunter, Falconer, Fowler and Fox.

Colours are also a source of popular surnames, as in Black, Brown, Gray/Grey, Green and White, and would have denoted the colour of the clothing the person habitually wore or, apart from the obvious exception of 'Green', one's hair colouring or even complexion.

The surname Red developed into Reid, while

Blue was rare and no-one wanted to be associated with yellow.

Rather self-important individuals took surnames that include Goodman and Wiseman, while physical attributes crept into surnames such as Small and Little.

Many families proudly boast the heraldic device known as a Coat of Arms, as featured on our front cover.

The central motif of the Coat of Arms would originally have been what was borne on the shield of a warrior to distinguish himself from others on the battlefield.

Not featured on the Coat of Arms, but highlighted on page three, is the family motto and related crest – with the latter frequently different from the central motif.

Adding further variety to the rich cultural heritage that is represented by surnames is the appearance in recent times in lists of the 100 most common names found in England of ones that include Khan, Patel and Singh – names that have proud roots in the vast sub-continent of India.

Echoes of a far distant past can still be found in our surnames and they can be borne with pride in commemoration of our forebears.

Chapter two:

Born free

A name of truly ancient historical roots, 'Freeman' derives from the Old English 'freomann' or 'friggmann' with 'freo' indicating 'free-born' while 'mann' is a now redundant spelling of 'man.'

'Freeman' therefore originally indicated 'free-born man', and was found as a forename before it became a surname.

'Freemen' were a class of workers or servants who lived under the system known as feudalism.

Although the term 'feudalism' was not coined by historians until the nineteenth century, it was a system that flourished throughout medieval Europe from about the ninth century AD until the middle of the fifteenth century.

With the vast majority of the population tied to the land, it was a system where status was defined by the labour or services required to be given to the owner of the land or manorial estate.

Lowest in the social classification were the serfs, who possessed practically no legal rights and lived in a form of abject slavery, subject to whatever demands their lord and master may have chosen to burden them with.

Enjoying greater freedom were the much smaller number of 'freemen', whose only obligation to their feudal lord was to pay him rent as tenant farmers.

'Villeins' meanwhile described the social class who, although renting land, were also required to spend some of their time working on their lords' fields and also providing military service when required.

Dissatisfaction with the harsh feudal system came to a head with the Peasants' Revolt of 1381.

Also known as the Great Rising or Wat Tyler's Rebellion, the revolt was a significant event in England's history, marking a dramatic turning point in the relationship between the rulers and the ruled.

But, although known as the Peasants' Revolt, it also had the support of a number of small landholders, or 'freemen' who objected to the haughty King Richard III's attempt to impose an early form of poll tax to further his costly foreign wars.

The revolt was sparked off in the summer of 1381 in the Essex villages of Brentwood and Fobbing.

When a king's representative attempted to

collect the hated poll tax, the villagers resisted his demands and sent the chastened would-be tax collector on his way.

Incensed by this flouting of the royal will, the king despatched Robert Belknap, Chief Justice of the Common Pleas, to the villages to punish his disobedient subjects.

He was promptly attacked by the villagers and forced to flee.

The revolt swiftly gathered momentum, spreading from Essex into Kent and East Anglia, with the Kentish rebels led by the charismatic Wat Tyler.

As the strength of the rebel forces swelled, they marched on London – assembling at Blackheath on June 12.

Various properties throughout the city were destroyed by the rebels over the next few days, while the Tower of London was stormed and a number of high-ranking officials, including Simon of Sudbury – the Archbishop of Canterbury and Lord Chancellor – summarily beheaded.

It was not until the king in person addressed a gathering of the rebels at Smithfield that the rebellion was defused – with the monarch promising to accede to their demands for reform.

But as the forces dispersed, he quickly reneged on his promises – hastily organising a 700-strong force of militia that hunted down and executed prominent rebel leaders and early champions of democracy who included Wat Tyler.

Although the revolt failed, the harsh lessons learned from it eventually led to slow, albeit reluctant, reform of the feudal system.

It was not until 1574 that the few remaining serfs in England were freed by order of Queen Elizabeth I.

Going much further back in time, the Freeman name itself is of ancient Anglo-Saxon roots – and flowing through the veins of many people of English birth today such as the Freemans is the blood of these Germanic tribes who invaded and settled in the south and east of the island of Britain from about the early fifth century.

Collectively known as the Anglo-Saxons, they were composed of the Jutes, from the area of the Jutland Peninsula in modern Denmark, the Saxons from Lower Saxony, in modern Germany and the Angles from the Angeln area of Germany.

It was the Angles who gave the name 'Engla land', or 'Aengla land' – better known as 'England.'

They held sway in what became known as England from approximately 550 to 1066, with the main kingdoms those of Sussex, Wessex, Northumbria, Mercia, Kent, East Anglia and Essex.

Through the Anglo-Saxons, the language known as Old English developed, later transforming from the eleventh century into Middle English – sources from which many popular English surnames of today, such as Freeman, derive.

A key event in English history is the Norman Conquest, which sounded the death knell of Anglo-Saxon supremacy.

By 1066, England had become a nation with several powerful competitors to the throne.

In what were extremely complex family, political and military machinations, the English monarch was Harold II, who had succeeded to the throne following the death of Edward the Confessor.

But his right to the throne was contested by two powerful competitors – his brother-in-law King Harold Hardrada of Norway, in alliance with Tostig, Harold II's brother, and Duke William II of Normandy.

In what has become known as The Year of

Three Battles, Hardrada invaded England and gained victory over the English king on September 20 at the battle of Fulford, in Yorkshire.

Five days later, however, Harold II decisively defeated his brother-in-law and brother at the battle of Stamford Bridge.

But Harold had little time to celebrate his victory, having to immediately march south from Yorkshire to encounter a mighty invasion force, led by Duke William of Normandy that had landed at Hastings, in East Sussex.

Harold's battle-hardened but exhausted force of Anglo-Saxon soldiers confronted the Normans on October 25.

It was at the top of Senlac Hill that Harold drew up a strong defensive position, building a shield wall to repel Duke William's cavalry and infantry.

The Normans suffered heavy losses, but through a combination of the deadly skill of their archers and the ferocious determination of their cavalry they eventually won the day.

Anglo-Saxon morale had collapsed on the battlefield as word spread through the ranks that Harold had been killed – the last of the Anglo-Saxon kings.

William was declared King of England on December 25, and the complete subjugation of his Anglo-Saxon subjects, such as the Freemans, followed.

Within an astonishingly short space of time, Norman manners, customs and law were imposed on England – laying the basis for what subsequently became established 'English' custom and practice.

But beneath the surface, old Anglo-Saxon culture was not totally eradicated.

Some aspects were absorbed into those of the Normans, while faint echoes of the Anglo-Saxon past is still seen today in the form of popular surnames such as Freeman.

Although the Freeman name was first found in Essex, it was not confined to this English county.

A William Freeman is recorded in Norfolk in 1196, while the name is also an Anglicised version of the Gaelic-Irish Mac antSoir, meaning 'son of the craftsman.'

The Freeman name figures prominently in the historical record.

Best known for his monumental *History of the Norman Conquest*, first published between 1867 and 1876 and which remains an important reference work to this day, Edward Freeman was the distinguished English historian born in 1823 in what is now the Birmingham suburb of Harborne.

His passion for history may have been fired through his own family history – tracing a maternal descent as he did from Colonel William Carless.

It was Colonel Carless who aided the future Charles II as he famously hid from his Parliamentary enemies in the branches of an oak tree after his defeat in 1651 at the battle of Worcester.

Before his death in 1892, Edward Freeman, who was also an architectural artist and British Liberal Party politician, held the post of Regius Professor of Modern History at Oxford University in addition to the post of non-resident professor at Cornell University, New York.

Chapter three:

Honours and distinction

**Bearers of the Freeman name have stamped their
mark on the historical record through a rich and
colourful range of pursuits and endeavours.**

One father and son of the name were
renowned structural engineers whose legacies survive
on the landscapes of a number of nations in the form
of some of the world's most impressive bridges.

Born in London in 1880, it was in 1901 that
Sir Ralph Freeman joined the firm of consulting
engineers Douglas Fox and Partners, which specialised
in the design of steel bridges.

By 1938, by which time Freeman was a
senior partner, the company became Freeman Fox and
Partners.

Best known for his design work on the Victoria
Falls Bridge, completed in 1905, he also designed the
Sydney Harbour Bridge, completed in 1935.

He died in 1950, while his son, also named
Ralph and who was also knighted for his contribution
to civil engineering, was responsible for the design of
the Humber Suspension Bridge, completed in 1981,

and at the time the longest single-span suspension bridge in the world.

Born in 1911, he was involved during the Second World War in the development of a special suspension bridge for military use.

British projects he was involved in after the war include the Severn Bridge, the Forth Road Bridge and the M2 and M5 motorways.

Serving for a time as president of the Institution of Civil Engineers, he died in 1998.

One noted American dynasty of Freemans was one founded by the millionaire James Stanley Freeman, born in 1874 in Jasper, Alabama.

Known as "Big Jim", he was one of the first to make a fortune through investments in New York's Wall Street – although before 1900 he twice made and then twice lost more than $1 million.

Following a much different career path than James Stanley Freeman, who died in 1960, his son James Shepherd Freeman was a famous admiral of the Second World War. Born in 1900 in Alabama and graduating from the United States Naval Academy in 1921, before the outbreak of war he served for a time as chief executive officer of the U.S. Naval Base at Pearl Harbor, Hawaii.

It was while commander of the *USS Alchiba* that in November of 1942 he was tasked with bringing supplies and ammunition to U.S. Marines stationed on Guadalcanal. Hit by torpedoes from two Japanese mini-submarines, Freeman ordered the engines turned to full throttle and ran the ship to shore.

By doing so, he not only saved the lives of his crew but also ensured that vital supplies were not lost.

Awarded the Military Cross for his actions, he died in 1962.

His son, James Shepherd Freeman, Jr., born in San Diego in 1926, attended the Naval Academy for only a short period before being discharged on medical grounds. He is better known for having been romantically linked for a time to the actress Shirley Temple and later as a senior executive of Union Carbide; he died in 1997.

Back to the fields of battle, John Freeman was an English recipient of the Victoria Cross (VC), the highest award for valour in the face of enemy action for British and Commonwealth forces.

Born in 1833 in Sittingbourne, Kent, he had been a private in the 9th Lancers (The Queen's Royals) during the Indian Mutiny when he performed the actions for which he was awarded the VC.

This was when, in October of 1857 at Agra, he went to the aid of a wounded officer who had been surrounded by the enemy and single-handedly managed to fight them off.

He died in 1913, while his VC is now on display at the Imperial War Museum, London.

Recognised as having played a vital role in the rearmament of the Royal Air Force (RAF) in the years leading up to, and during, the Second World War, Sir Wilfred Freeman was born in 1888.

Seeing service during the First World War with the Royal Flying Corps – forerunner of the RAF – he later served as commandant of the Central Flying School and commandant of the RAF Staff College.

It was in 1936 that he was entrusted with choosing the aircraft with which the RAF badly needed to rearm.

This led to the RAF being supplied with a range of aircraft that included the Supermarine Spitfire and Hawker Hurricane fighters and the Avro Lancaster and Handley-Page Halifax bombers.

Later serving as Vice-Chief of the Air Staff and having been honoured with a Baronetcy in the Peerage of the United Kingdom, he died in 1953.

Back across the Atlantic from Britain, Paul

Lamarch Freeman was the United States Army four-star general born in 1907 in the Philippine Islands.

Graduating from the United States Military Academy in 1929 and commissioned in the infantry, he went on to serve in senior command posts that included Commander in Chief, U.S. Army Europe from 1962 to 1965 and, from 1965 to 1967, Commanding General, U.S. Continental Army Command. The recipient of many awards and honours that include the Distinguished Service Cross, Army Distinguished Service Medal and the Legion of Merit, he died in 1988.

In the field of medicine, Walter Freeman II was the American physician who pioneered work in neurological science. Controversially, this involved carrying out more than 200 lobotomy procedures on mentally disturbed patients between 1936 and 1942.

Born in Philadelphia in 1895, he died in 1972. Despite the controversy surrounding his career he is nevertheless recognised as having made important contributions to the fields of both neurology and psychiatry.

He was the father of Walter Freeman III, the distinguished biologist, neuroscientist and philosopher born in 1927 in Washington, D.C.

A teacher of brain science at the University of California since 1959, his many honours include a 1990 National Institute of Mental Health Award.

In the world of international diplomacy, Charles Freeman, born in 1943, is the American diplomat who most notably served as President Richard M. Nixon's main interpreter during his 1972 visit to China and, from 1989 to 1992, as United States Ambassador to Saudi Arabia.

A past president of the Middle East Policy Council, he has also served as vice-chair of the U.S. China Policy Foundation and as vice-chair of the Atlantic Council.

One particularly intrepid bearer of the Freeman name was the American explorer, war correspondent and author Lewis Freeman, born in 1878 in Genoa Junction, Wisconsin.

Moving with his family as a child to Pasadena, California, he later attended Stanford University where, in addition to his academic work, he excelled not only in baseball and football but also in athletics and tennis.

Following his graduation, he spent from 1899 to 1912 travelling throughout his native North America, South America, the Pacific Islands and

Africa – also serving for a time as a newspaper war correspondent during the Russo-Japanese War of 1904 to 1905.

The First World War also saw him serving as a war correspondent, while at the end of the conflict he was appointed a staff member of the Inter-Allied Naval Armistice Commission.

Acting as a photographer for a U.S. Geological Survey expedition through the Grand Canyon in 1923, he spent from 1930 to 1931 as a member of an aeroplane and motorboat expedition to Central and South America.

Further expeditions included one to the head-waters of the Amazon and Ecuador, while in 1941 he explored Brazil, Peru and Bolivia.

Another of his noted feats had been six years earlier when he rode a bicycle coast to coast in North America from Los Angeles to Vancouver, then from Vancouver to Montreal and from there to New York City.

Author of a number of books that include his 1918 *Many Fronts*, the 1927 *Waterways of Westward Wandering* and the 1942 *Brazil, Land of Tomorrow* and also a member of the Explorers Club in New York City, he died in 1960.

Chapter four:

On the world stage

A mechanic with the United States Air Force before moving to Los Angeles in the early 1960s and taking to the stage with theatre groups, Morgan Freeman is the American actor and film director born in 1937 in Memphis, Tennessee.

The recipient of an Academy Award for Best Actor for his role in the 2004 *Million Dollar Baby*, he also received nominations for the 1987 *Street Smart*, the 1989 *Driving Miss Daisy*, the 1994 *The Shawshank Redemption* and, from 2009, *Invictus*.

Other screen credits include the 1989 *Glory*, the 2002 *The Sum of All Fears* and the 2012 *The Dark Knight Rises*.

Cast in the lead role of Bilbo Baggins in New Zealand film director Peter Jackson's planned three-part adaptation of J.R. Tolkien's *The Hobbit*, **Martin Freeman** is the English actor born in 1971 in Aldershot.

The first in the series, *The Hobbit: An Unexpected Journey*, was released in 2012, while at the time of writing *The Hobbit: There and Back Again* is planned for release in 2013.

Also known for his role as Tim Canterbury in the BBC television sitcom *The Office* and as Dr Watson in *Sherlock*, other big screen credits include the 2003 *Love Actually* and the 2005 film adaptation of Douglas Adams' *The Hitchhiker's Guide to the Galaxy*.

Known for her role from 2008 to 2011 as Tess Mercer in the television drama *Smallville*, **Cassidy Freeman** is the American actress born in 1982 in Chicago.

Other television credits include *CSI: Crime Scene Investigation* and the 2012 *The Vampire Diaries*, while big screen credits include the 2006 *Razor*.

Nominated in 1994 for a Tony Award for Best Performance by a Featured Actor in a Musical for his role in *She Loves Me*, **Jonathan Freeman** is the American actor born in 1950 in Cleveland, Ohio.

In addition to having appeared on Broadway revival productions that include *The Producers*, *42nd Street* and *On the Town*, he is also known as the 'voice' of the villain Jafar in Disney's 1992 *Aladdin*.

Married to the English actress Maggie Scot, with whom he co-starred in the 1981 film *The Dogs of War*, **Paul Freeman** is the actor born in 1943 in Barnet, Herefordshire.

Other screen credits include the 1980 *The Long Good Friday* and the 1981 *Raiders of the Lost Ark*.

Behind the camera lens, **Dave Freeman**, born in 1922, was the British television and film writer who, in addition to writing sketches for comedians who included Arthur Askey and Tony Hancock, also wrote screenplays for films that include the 1976 *Jules Verne's Rocket to the Moon*, the 1975 *Carry on Behind* and the 1992 *Columbus*.

Also a writer for the comedian Benny Hill, he died in 2005.

Born in 1916 in Spokane, Washington, **John H. Freeman** was the character animator for Disney who, over a period of sixteen years, was involved in films that include the 1940 *Fantasia*, the 1953 *Peter Pan* and, from 1955, *The Lady and the Tramp*; he died in 2010.

Noted for films that include his 1997 *Hurricane Streets* – winner of three Sundance Film Festival awards – the 1998 *Desert Blue* and the 2009 *Homecoming*, **Morgan J. Freeman** is the film director born in 1969 in Long Beach, California.

From film to music, **Alan Freeman** was the disc jockey and radio personality also known by his nickname of "Fluff."

Born in 1927 in Victoria, Australia, he turned his back on a career as an accountant in favour of radio.

Working for a time as a presenter for a Tasmanian radio station, he moved to London in 1957 and later worked for Radio Luxembourg followed by a number of BBC stations that include Radio One.

Known for catchphrases that included "Greeting, pop pickers" and "Alright? Stay bright!" and the recipient in 2000 of a Lifetime Achievement Award at the Sony Radio Academy Awards, he died in 2006.

In the world of art, **Robert Freeman** is the British designer and photographer best known for having created the photographic art work for a number of Beatles albums that include *With the Beatles*, *Beatles for Sale*, *Help* and *Rubber Soul*.

In the sciences, **Hans Charles Freeman** was the German-born Australian chemist who was a pioneer in the fields of bio-inorganic chemistry and crystallography.

Born into a Jewish family in Breslau in 1929,

they moved to Australia in 1938 to escape Nazi persecution.

Undertaking most of his research at the University of Sydney, a Fellow of the Australian Academy of Sciences and Member of the Order of Australia, he died in 2008.

Bearers of the Freeman name have also excelled, and continue to excel, in the highly competitive world of sport.

On the athletics track, and recognised as having been one of the greatest female sprinters of all time, **Cathy Freeman** was born in 1973 in Queensland, Australia.

Specialising in the 400-metres event, she was aged 16 when she became the first Aboriginal Commonwealth Games medallist.

Winner of the silver medal in the 400-metres sprint at the 1996 Olympics in Atlanta, she won gold four years later at the Sydney Olympics.

Also the winner of other major championships that include the 1999 World Championships, she retired from athletics in 2003.

Her many awards and honours include 1998 Australian of the Year, the Medal of the Order of Australia and the Olympic Order.

From the athletics track to the cricket pitch, Percy Freeman, better known as **Tich Freeman**, was a renowned English cricketer of the early twentieth century.

Born in 1888 in Lewisham, London, and nicknamed "Tich" because of his 5ft. 2in. stature, and a leg spin bowler for Kent and England, his many records include taking 1,673 wickets in six consecutive seasons from 1928 to 1933.

His Test debut was against Australia in 1924, while his last was in 1929 against South Africa.

Recognised to this day as one of the most prolific wicket takers in first class cricket history, he died in 1965.

In baseball, John Frank Freeman, better known as **Buck Freeman**, was a leading figure in the sport.

Born in 1871 in Catasauqua, Pennsylvania, and playing as a right fielder between 1891 and 1907 for teams that included the Washington Statesmen/Senators, Boston Beaneaters and Boston Americans, it was in the 1899 season that he hit 25 home runs.

The recipient of many awards and honours that include 1903 World Champion while playing for the Boston Americans, he died in 1949.

In the equally popular sport of American football, **Antonio Freeman**, born in 1972 in Baltimore, Maryland, is the former wide receiver of the National Football League (NFL) who played for teams that include the Green Bay Packers, Philadelphia Eagles and Miami Dolphins.

A member of the Green Bay Packers Hall of Fame, he is now a television pundit on the game.

In the rough and tumble that is the game of rugby league, **Gary Freeman** is the New Zealand former player who earned 37 caps playing for his country between 1986 and 1995.

Having played for teams that include Northcote Tigers, Paramatta Eels and Castleford Tigers, he was also a coach for the New Zealand team from 2001 to 2002.

A Member of the New Zealand Order of Merit for his services to rugby league, he is also an inductee of the New Zealand Rugby League's 'Legends of League' roll of honour.

One particularly creative bearer of the proud name of Freeman was the novelist Richard Austin Freeman, better known as **R. Austin Freeman**.

Born in London in 1862, he is recognised as having introduced what is known as the 'inverted detective story' – in which the commission of the crime and the identity of the perpetrator are revealed to readers at the beginning of the tale, with the rest of the novel describing the detective's attempts to solve the crime.

It was because of ill health that he turned to writing.

Qualifying as a medical doctor in 1887, he worked for a time as a colonial surgeon in Accra, on the Gold Coast, before being forced to return to British shores suffering from the debilitating effects of blackwater fever.

Unable to secure a full-time medical position, he took up the pen and created the character of the forensic investigator Dr Thorndyke, utilising the 'inverted detective' technique.

The first in his series of Dr Thorndyke novels, the 1907 *The Red Thumb Mark*, proved a great success, and Freeman went one to produce one book almost every year until his death in 1943.